W9-APJ-339

Earl Pritchett School
200 Horatio Blvd.
Buffalo Grove, IL 60089

FROM SEA to SHINING SEA

ILLINOIS

BARBARA A. SOMERVILL

Consultants

MELISSA N. MATUSEVICH, PH.D.
Curriculum and Instruction Specialist
Blacksburg, Virginia

PATRICIA A. DEMPSEY
Library Media Coordinator
Blaine Elementary, Chicago Public Schools
Chicago, Illinois

CHILDREN'S PRESS®
A DIVISION OF SCHOLASTIC INC.

New York • Toronto • London • Auckland • Sydney • Mexico City
New Delhi • Hong Kong • Danbury, Connecticut

Illinois is bordered by Missouri, Iowa, Wisconsin, Indiana, and Kentucky.

Project Editor: Lewis K. Parker
Art Director: Marie O'Neill
Photo Researcher: Marybeth Kavanagh
Design: Robin West, Ox and Company, Inc.
Page 6 map and recipe art: Susan Hunt Yule
All other maps: XNR Productions, Inc.

Library of Congress Cataloging in-Publication Data
Somervill, Barbara A.
        Illinois/by Barbara A. Somervill
            p. cm.—(From sea to shining sea)
        Includes bibliographical references and index.
        ISBN 0-516-22320-8
Illinois—Juvenile literature. [1. Illinois.] I. Title. II. From sea to shining sea (Series)

F541.3 .S66 2001
977.3—dc21   00-065959

TABLE of CONTENTS

CHAPTER ONE

INTRODUCING THE PRAIRIE STATE

The statue of Lincoln is illuminated in front of the capitol building.

When you think of Illinois, what ideas pop into your mind? Do you think of bustling, busy Chicago? Or do you think about broad, sweeping plains, covered with tall grass and wildflowers and dotted with small towns? Surprisingly, Illinois is both! Chicago is Illinois's largest city with over seven million people. The state also has some really small towns—Bentley, Muddy, and Union Hill each have fewer than one hundred people.

Illinois is called the Prairie State because almost all of the land was once covered by prairie, which is flat or rolling grassland. Another nickname for Illinois is "the Land of Lincoln." Abraham Lincoln worked as a lawyer in Springfield. He owned a home in that city and was elected president while living in the state.

The state's seal features an eagle in its center, along with a red, white, and blue shield that represents the United States. In its beak, the eagle carries a ribbon with the words "State Sovereignty, National Union" written on it. During the Civil War, when some states wanted to separate from the United States, the words on the seal were reversed to say "National Union, State Sovereignty."

What can you find in Illinois?

- Places that honor Abraham Lincoln—
  you can visit his home and his tomb
- Amish people driving their buggies
- Chefs serving famous Chicago deep-dish pizza
- Chicago Bears players charging down the field
- Metropolis, the hometown of Superman
- Hippos and crocodiles at the Brookfield Zoo
- Kids blowing bubbles in front of the Wrigley Building

Illinois is farms and cities, and plenty of people. It is rich in history and heritage. As you read this book, you will learn all about the marvelous state of Illinois—the Prairie State.

Wisconsin

Freeport. Rockford

WRIGLEY

LAKE
MICHIGAN

Iowa

Chicago

Peoria

MISSISSIPPI RIVER

Urbana

Springfield

Missouri

©SHY01

Indiana

•Carbondale

Metropolis

Kentucky

CHAPTER TWO

THE LAND OF ILLINOIS

Illinois is a "middle" state. It is in the middle of the country, and it is in the middle in size. Overall, Illinois is 57,354 square miles (148,546 square kilometers), and ranks twenty-fourth in size of all the states. Of that total area, land covers 54,877 square miles (142,131 sq km), and 2,477 square miles (6,415 sq km) are inland water.

To the west of Illinois, the Mississippi River draws the border between Illinois and its neighbors, Missouri and Iowa. Along the north, the state shares a border with Wisconsin. Lake Michigan provides a border to the northeast. Indiana lies to the east and Kentucky to the southeast. Illinois is 381 miles (613 km) long from north to south, and 211 miles (340 km) wide.

Illinois has three geographic regions: the Central Plains, the Shawnee Hills, and the Gulf Coastal Plains. The Central Plains cover almost ninety percent of the state. The soil in this region is dark, rich, and ideal

This photo shows Camel Rock at the Garden of the Gods Recreation Area. This recreation area is located in the Shawnee Hills.

Farmers using a combine harvester reap a field of soybeans.

EXTRA! EXTRA!

Shawnee National Forest is Illinois's only national forest. It is in the southern area of the state. Hikers enjoy the Ozark-Shawnee Trail which crosses through the forest.

for farming. Illinois's citizens call this area the "Garden Spot of the Nation." Farmers grow corn, wheat, and vegetables here.

The highest point in Illinois, Charles Mound (1,235 feet or 376 meters), is found in the hill country near the Wisconsin border. This area is filled with hills, valleys, and ridges.

The Great Lakes Plains, a section of the Central Plains, cover the northeast section of the state, from Wisconsin to the Indiana border. More than a million years ago, much of this area was part of Lake Michigan. As the lake drew back from the land, it left behind rich soil and marshland. Many parts of Chicago, which is in this area, were built on a swamp.

Throughout the state, only about eleven percent of the land is covered by forest, and that land is largely in the Shawnee Hills. This region carves a narrow band along the bottom of the state. The area is hilly, with sharp bluffs or cliffs dropping down to the Wabash River. At the southern point of the Shawnee Hills, the Wabash meets the Ohio River. As settlers moved into the Shawnee Hills, they discovered the area was ideal for growing peaches and apples. The Shawnee Hills are Illinois's fruit basket.

At the bottom tip of Illinois is a small region called the Gulf Coastal Plains. Weather patterns in the Gulf Coastal Plains—rain, snow, and clear skies—flow up the Mississippi River Valley from the Gulf of Mexico, far to the south.

These people are exploring a trail in the Shawnee National Forest in the southern area of the state.

The Ohio River flows into the Mississippi in the Gulf Coastal Plains. You'll find the lowest point in Illinois along the Mississippi (279 feet or 85 m) near where these two rivers join. Because both the Mississippi and Ohio have flooded many times, the area is more like a river delta, just as you would find at the mouth of the Mississippi. The land is covered with rich soil deposited by the rivers during flooding. Although the soil is good for farming, farmers often fear that their crops may be destroyed by heavy floods.

Bald cypress and tupelo trees grow in an Illinois lake.

RIVERS AND LAKES

Illinois has more than five hundred rivers and streams and 2,915 lakes and reservoirs. The longest river is the Illinois River (273 miles or 439 km), which flows into the Mississippi. Other large rivers in the state

FIND OUT MORE

A delta is the land formed at the mouth of a river. The Greek capital letter *delta* looks like this: Δ . How might this landform have received its name?

Many people enjoy riding boats on the Chicago River.

include the Chicago River, the Des Plaines, the Kankakee, the Sangamon, and the Fox.

At one time the Chicago River flowed into Lake Michigan. When Europeans first came to present-day Chicago, the water was so pure that they could drink from it. By the 1850s, this river was badly polluted, and the river's fish had died. In 1900, engineers built a system of locks to change the river's flow from eastward to westward. The state legislature also passed anti-pollution laws that helped clean up the Chicago River. Today, more than thirty types of fish live in this river.

Most of Illinois's lakes, including Lake Michigan, were formed by glaciers. Thousands of years ago, glaciers covered most of present-day Illinois. When the glaciers moved, they dug hollows in the ground. Later, as the glaciers melted, these hollows filled with water and formed lakes. The Chain O'Lakes along the state's northern border is a popular recreation area. Reservoirs as the result of dams form the state's largest lakes. These include Carlyle Lake (26,000 acres or 10,500 hectares), Rend Lake, Crab Orchard Lake, Lake Decatur, and Lake Springfield.

Only about ten percent of Illinois is covered with forest. Common trees include hickory, maple, oak, walnut, and cottonwood. The rest of Illinois is prairie, with more than three hundred different types of grass. Some of this grass can grow as high as six feet (2 m) tall. Illinois's nickname, the Prairie State, comes from these beautiful prairies.

Many kinds of wildflowers sprinkle their bright colors throughout the woodland. One of these is the native violet, the state flower. Other common wildflowers have such interesting names as bloodroot, dogtooth violets, toothwort, and Dutchman's-breeches.

Because there is not much forest to provide habitat, few large game animals live in Illinois. Common animals are the white-tailed deer, beavers, foxes, minks, muskrats, rabbits, squirrels, raccoons, and skunks. Illinois is the winter home of millions of ducks and thousands of Canada geese, snow geese, and blue geese. The state has preserves such as the Squaw Creek Natural Preserve and Grass Lake Preserve where these birds may find safety.

Blazing stars and rattlesnake masters are two kinds of wildflowers growing in this prairie field.

FIND OUT MORE

Northern Illinois receives about thirty inches (76 centimeters) of snow a year. This snowfall only amounts to one to two inches of precipitation. Why do you think that more than two feet (.61m) of snow equals so little precipitation?

CLIMATE

Illinois has cold winters and hot summers. The average July temperature in Illinois is 76°F (24°C). The hottest recorded temperature was 117°F (47°C) on July 14, 1954, at East St. Louis. During the winter, average

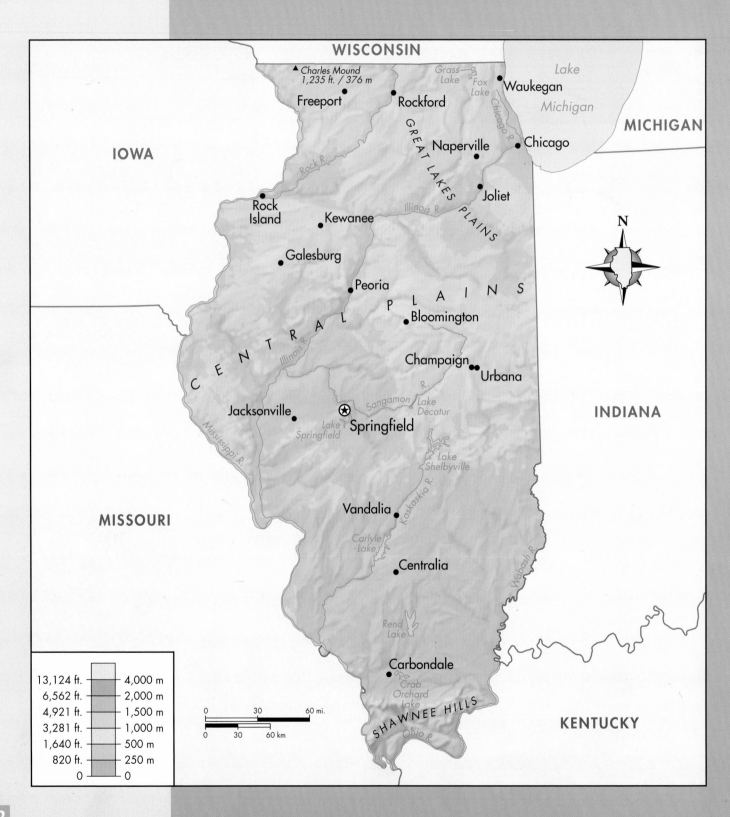

WISCONSIN

▲ Charles Mound
1,235 ft. / 376 m

Freeport

Rockford

Grass Lake

Fox Lake

Waukegan

Lake

Michigan

MICHIGAN

IOWA

Chicago R.

Naperville

Chicago

G R E A T   L A K E S   P L A I N S

Rock Island

Kewanee

Illinois R.

Joliet

Rock R.

Galesburg

Peoria

C E N T R A L   P L A I N S

Bloomington

N

Illinois R.

Champaign

Urbana

INDIANA

Jacksonville

Sangamon R.

Lake Decatur

⊛ Springfield

Lake Springfield

Mississippi R.

Lake Shelbyville

MISSOURI

Vandalia

Kaskaskia R.

Carlyle Lake

Wabash R.

Centralia

Rend Lake

Carbondale

Crab Orchard Lake

S H A W N E E   H I L L S

Ohio R.

KENTUCKY

13,124 ft.	4,000 m
6,562 ft.	2,000 m
4,921 ft.	1,500 m
3,281 ft.	1,000 m
1,640 ft.	500 m
820 ft.	250 m
0	0

0   30   60 mi.

0   30   60 km

When violent storms strike, the clouds seem to hover right over the flat land.

temperatures dip to 27°F (–3°C). The coldest day in Illinois was an icy –36°F (–38°C) at Congerville, on January 5, 1999.

Most precipitation (rain, snow, sleet, and hail) in Illinois comes from the Gulf of Mexico. It is carried on winds up the Mississippi River Valley. Southern Illinois records about forty-six inches (117 cm) of precipitation per year. Northern Illinois gets about thirty-six inches (91 cm) of precipitation.

EXTRA! EXTRA!

Illinois gets its share of dangerous tornadoes. In fact, more people are killed by tornadoes in Illinois than in any other state. Since 1916, tornadoes have resulted in the deaths of about 1,000 people in Illinois.

CHAPTER THREE

ILLINOIS THROUGH HISTORY

Early Native American villages were often temporary. When the main food supply—herds of animals—moved on, so did the hunters.

The first people arrived in present-day Illinois around 10,000 years ago. They were called Paleo-Indians. They lived in the forests or in caves along river bluffs. They hunted large animals, such as giant buffalo and woolly mammoths. These people also survived by eating berries, nuts, and roots. Scientists know very little about them. All that is left to study of the Paleo-Indians are some remains of their way of life—stone spearheads and the fossilized bones of animals they ate.

Scientists do not know what happened to the Paleo-Indians. However, about three thousand years ago they vanished, and other people moved into today's Illinois. These people are called the Woodland people and the Hopewell people. Both groups lived in small villages. They were farmers who made hoes from flint, and grew corn, pumpkin, squash, and beans. The Hopewell people made pottery for storing food, carrying water, and cooking. For hunting, they made bows and arrows.

These groups were also "mound builders." They carried soil and heaped it up to form mounds. They used some of these huge earthen mounds for burying their dead. Temples were built on other mounds and they were used for religious events. Many mounds still exist across the United States. For example, Monk's Mound, near East St. Louis, is the largest native-built mound in North America, covering seventeen acres of land. This mound is near the center of the ruins of a city where scientists believe about 100,000 people once lived. That's a city about the size of Clearwater, Florida; Berkeley, California; or Stamford, Connecticut—built more than one thousand years ago.

Just as with the Paleo-Indians, there is no clear reason why the mound builders disappeared. By 1500, the mound builders were gone, and new native tribes had moved into the area. These tribes included the Illiniwek, the Kaskaskia, the Chippewa, and the Iroquois. Some native people came on foot, while others came in canoes hollowed out of birch trees. These people lived in organized clans or tribes, hunted and fished, and grew vegetables.

This drawing shows an Illiniwek Indian. The Illiniwek lost their land to Iroquois invaders and European settlers.

EUROPEANS ARRIVE

The first Europeans to arrive in today's Illinois were Jacques Marquette and Louis Jolliet in 1673. These French explorers traveled down the Mississippi as far as present-day Arkansas. On their return trip, they

Jacques Marquette and Louis Jolliet were the first Europeans in Illinois.

traveled up the Illinois River. This is believed to be the first contact between Illinois Native Americans and Europeans.

Marquette had once lived with native tribes in Canada and could talk with the tribes living in Illinois using different forms of Algonquian, a native language. Marquette and other French travelers called the region *Illinois.* The name Illinois is a French version of Illiniwek, who were a local native tribe. The name itself means either "strong men" or "the people." The French combined *illini* and the French suffix *ois* to form the name Illinois.

By the 1670s when Marquette and Jolliet arrived, there were about sixty Illiniwek villages, with about 10,000 people, in the area. The Illiniwek had formed a nation from several smaller tribes, including the Cahokia, the Peoria, the Michigamea, the Moingwena, and the Tamarou.

Several other tribes also lived in present-day Illinois—the Potawatomi, the Santee Sioux, the Fox, the Sauk, and the Winnebago. These tribes did not all get along well. They fought with each other over land and hunting territory. The Iroquois, a group of native people from the New York area, came from the east and also fought against the Illiniwek. The arrival of Europeans meant the arrival of deadly diseases, such as smallpox, chicken pox, measles, and bubonic plague. Illinois's Native Americans could not fight each other, the Europeans, and diseases, too.

As Illinois's Native American population decreased, the French took control of Illinois. In 1675, Marquette set up a mission at the Great Village of the Illinois near present-day Utica. In 1680, René Robert Cavelier, Sieur de La Salle, and Henri de Tonti introduced fur trading to the area. The French trapped fur-bearing animals,

Fur trading became an important business for French trappers.

La Salle explored throughout the Mississippi River Valley.

such as beaver and fox. They traded food, tools, and liquor with the Native Americans for furs. These furs were sold in the East or in Europe for large sums of money.

La Salle and de Tonti set up Fort Crèvecoeur along the Illinois River. This fort became a central trading post for the region. De Tonti, who had lost a hand in a naval battle and wore a metal hook in its place, fascinated the local Native Americans. The natives called him "iron hand."

During the next twenty years, the French continued to build in Illinois. Fort St. Louis, Guardian Angel mission at present-day Chicago, and Holy Family mission at Cahokia were all built during this time period. Holy Family mission became the first permanent European settlement in Illinois. For one hundred years, French settlements grew in both number and size. The French got along well with the local Native Americans, as they respected the land and the native way of life. The French worked side-by-side with local native people. The same could not be said of the British, who wanted native land and were willing to fight for it.

THE BRITISH TAKE OVER

From 1754 to 1763, the French and British fought over land and trading rights in North America. This was the French and Indian War, with the British on one side, fighting against the French troops and many native tribes on the other side. After nine years of fighting, the British and French signed a treaty to end the war. The treaty, called the Treaty of Paris, gave all land east of the Mississippi River, including Illinois, to the British.

The French and Indian War was very expensive for the British. They had sent troops from England for fighting. They had to pay their soldiers, as well as provide food, clothing, and weapons. In Great Britain, the government decided that the colonies in North America should pay the costs of the war. The British government began taxing the colonies through the Stamp Act, the Townshend Act, the Quartering Act, and other taxes. The colonists paid tax on everything from stamps, books, and tea to glass windows and playing cards. The colonists were angered by the taxes and by the way Great Britain treated their colonies.

In 1773, Boston citizens rebelled against British taxes. In an event called the "Boston Tea Party," heavily-taxed tea was tossed into Boston Harbor. This was only one of many small acts against the British. In 1775 the Continental Congress met and named George Washington Commander-in-chief of the Continental Army. The American Revolution (1775–1783) began, and the colonists fought for their freedom from Great Britain.

EXTRA! EXTRA!

A mission is a place where people teach religion or start schools or hospitals. French missions in Illinois were started to teach natives about Roman Catholicism.

People in Kaskaskia were surprised when George Rogers Clark and his army arrived.

Although much of the American Revolution took place in the eastern colonies, Illinois played its part in the war. For example, the British held the town of Kaskaskia, on the Mississippi River. In 1778, George Rogers Clark led a group of Kentucky volunteers to Kaskaskia and took over the town. At that time, Illinois country became a part of Virginia.

The Revolutionary War came to an end in 1783, and the United States began governing itself. In 1787, the U.S. Congress passed a law called the Northwest Ordinance, which established the Northwest Territory. This territory included the land of Illinois, Wisconsin, Ohio, Indiana, and Michigan. In 1809, the U.S. Congress set up the separate territory of Illinois. Kaskaskia became the capital, and Ninian Edwards was named the territorial governor.

The Illinois Territory continued growing. More people moved into the area, setting up farms and building towns. By 1818, the territory had a thriving economy and people were looking toward a bright future.

In order for a territory to become a state, the territory needed to have a population of 60,000. Even though the population was only 35,000 people at the time, Illinois Territory applied to the U.S. Congress to

FIND OUT MORE

Today, we think of the Northwest as Idaho, Washington, and Oregon. Why do you think Illinois, Wisconsin, Ohio, Indiana, and Michigan were called "the Northwest Territory"?

Fort Dearborn was built in 1803. In 1812, Potawatomi Indians attacked and burned the fort.

become a state. Although the Illinois Territory was 25,000 people short of the required population figure, Congress granted statehood. Illinois became the twenty-first state on December 3, 1818. The first governor of Illinois was Shadrack Bond.

AFTER STATEHOOD

Kaskaskia, located on the Mississippi, remained the capital city of Illinois. However, the Mississippi River often flooded the town, so, in 1820, the capital was changed to Vandalia, a city that was farther inland. Vandalia would not remain the capital for long, however. By 1839, the state legislature had selected Springfield as the state capital.

The state grew fast as pioneers began moving from the East to Illinois. However, farmers found that prairie soil was very hard—so hard that it broke iron or wooden plows. In 1837, a man named John Deere made a new steel plow that solved the farmers' problems. His plow could cut easily through the hard soil and tangled roots of the prairie.

It was not easy living in Illinois in those days. Pioneer days began at dawn—chores included chopping wood, cooking over open fires, hauling water, tending farm animals, and planting fields. Families ate bread, hominy (mush made from dried corn), and small game such as rabbit, squirrel, or opossum.

In the early 1830s, one problem that pioneers faced was disease. Diseases such as cholera, typhoid fever, and malaria killed men, women, and children alike. Children also suffered from whooping cough and

The steel plow invented by John Deere made it much easier for farmers to turn the Illinois soil.

diphtheria. Some children died of an odd condition called "milk sick," from drinking the milk of cows that ate poisonous weeds.

Another problem for pioneers concerned Native Americans. Settlers were taking land that belonged to Native American tribes. As more and more settlers moved into Illinois, many tribes were forced to move to Iowa, on land so poor that they could not grow enough crops to feed their people.

In 1832, a Native American named Black Hawk led Sauk warriors into Illinois to try to gain their land back. Army troops,

FIND OUT MORE

Whooping cough and diphtheria were once deadly for children. Most people today have never heard of "milk sick." Why do you think that most children no longer suffer from whooping cough, diphtheria, or milk sick?

This drawing shows a battle during the Black Hawk War.

far outnumbering the native warriors, fought against them. The "Black Hawk War" lasted four months. Many of Black Hawk's band were killed, and Black Hawk eventually surrendered and settled in Iowa.

THE MORMONS IN ILLINOIS

In 1839, Joseph Smith, founder of the Church of Latter Day Saints (the Mormons), led his followers to a new town called Nauvoo, on the Mississippi River, due west of Peoria. The Mormons built a large settlement, making plans for schools, a temple, and a hotel. Many Illinoisans were jealous of the Mormons' success. They were also angered by the Mormon practice that allowed men to have more than one wife. Between 1844 and 1846, the Mormons were tormented by Illinois citizens. On June 27, 1844, an angry mob killed Joseph Smith and his brother Hyrum. Within the next two years, most Mormons had left Illinois for Utah.

An artist captured this scene of the Lincoln-Douglas debate at Galesburg in 1858.

THE CIVIL WAR

In 1858, Abraham Lincoln and Stephen A. Douglas both wanted to be elected to the U.S. Senate from Illinois. At the time, Lincoln was a lawyer in Springfield. Douglas was in favor of westward expansion and allowing territories to decide their own future. Lincoln thought that slavery should not spread into the new territories. At the time, many southern states "owned" African-Americans and put them to work on plantations. Slaves were not paid wages and were treated as property that was bought and sold. Slavery was less common, but still present, in the North.

Lincoln and Douglas met in a series of debates (public discussions) over the future of Illinois and the United States. Lincoln lost the Senate election, but the debates between Lincoln and Douglas became famous. Two years later, Lincoln was elected the sixteenth U.S. President. Slavery and the right of people who lived in the states to decide their own way of life were very important issues when Lincoln was elected.

In addition to holding different views concerning slavery, people in the northern states and in the southern states led very different ways of life. The North was mainly industrial—many people in these states made their living by manufacturing products. They worked in factories or mills and were paid wages. The Southern states had some factories, but most people made their living by farming. There were many small farms, but large farms called plantations were common. Plantations produced one main product—usually cotton or tobacco. African-American slaves did much of the hard work on plantations.

Many people in the Southern states feared that Lincoln would end slavery, which was important to the Southern economy. They worried that new states joining the United States would not be allowed to have slavery. This would mean more "free" states than "slave" states, which would reduce the power of the Southern states in the U.S. Congress. Many people in the Southern states did not want a federal government that was more powerful than individual states.

Shortly after the 1860 election, states in the South began to secede, or withdraw, from the United States. They formed a new country called the Confederate States of America. In April 1861, Confederate troops attacked Fort Sumter in South Carolina in an effort to remove the Union (northern) presence. The Civil War (1861–1865) had begun.

Illinois sent about 260,000 men to fight in the Civil War on the Union side. The state sent beef and grain to the army, and lead for bullets. Cairo, Illinois, became a supply depot for shipping food and ammunition, and an army base during the war. In all, Illinois fared better than most states during the war. No battles were fought on Illinois soil. About 35,000 Illinois soldiers died,

less than that of other Union states. In April 1865, the Confederate Army surrendered and the sothern states were eventually admitted back into the Union.

THE CHICAGO FIRE

After the Civil War, Illinois continued to grow. Chicago became a manufacturing and transportation center for the Midwest. However, disaster struck the city on October 8, 1871. A fire started in a barn in the southern end of Chicago. The fire, pushed by high winds, spread quickly because most of the buildings in town were made of wood.

Ada Rumsey, a child living in Chicago, described the night of the fire: "The sky kept getting red and redder; the wind, already high, was

There was panic in the streets as thousands first tried to watch, then escape, the Great Chicago Fire.

increasing with the heat, and huge burning cinders were settling from every direction. . . . Houses were burning about us and our own house was on fire. The streets were filled with vehicles loaded with household goods and with people staggering under big loads."

Within one day, about 20,000 buildings burned to the ground. About three hundred people died, and over 100,000 were left homeless. Yet, Chicago rose out of the ashes of that fire and was rebuilt within just two or three years.

During the late 1800s, wars, famine, and a desire for freedom made many people in Europe decide to move to the United States. Immigrants from Ireland, Germany, and Poland poured into Illinois. By 1880, almost half of Illinois's population was foreign-born. With these immigrants came the foods, music, and culture of their homelands.

Life in Illinois was not easy for new immigrants. Many people found hard work in meatpacking houses, factories, and steel mills. Workdays were long. Men, women, and children often worked from twelve to fourteen hours a day, six days a week—and workplaces were dangerous. Workers in packing plants often received deep cuts or lost fingers or hands in unsafe machinery. Some people received infections from handling raw meat. Steel mill workers had no protection from being burned by molten steel.

In an effort to demand better conditions, many workers formed labor unions. In 1884, the Illinois State Federation of Labor, a group of unions, met in Chicago. One change that the unions wanted was an eight-hour workday.

Throughout the late 1880s, unions struggled against business owners by holding strikes (refusing to work). Business owners didn't want to accept the demands

WHAT'S IN A NAME?

Many names of places in Illinois have interesting origins.

Name	Source/Meaning
Illinois	French version of *illiniwek*, meaning "strong men"
Kaskaskia	The name of a native tribe in southwestern Illinois
Carbondale	For the coal (carbon) mined in the region
Half Day	Supposedly because it took a "half day" to get there from Chicago
Lincoln	In honor of President Abraham Lincoln
Des Plaines	French for "of the plains"
Nauvoo	After the Hebrew word for "beautiful place"

made by unions and sometimes they reacted in violent ways. In 1886 the Haymarket Riot rocked Chicago. The roots of the riot started with a strike against the McCormick Reaper Company. Workers wanted an eight-hour day. The strike became violent and six workers were killed. The next night, protestors met at Haymarket Square. At first the meeting was peaceful. When police tried to break up the meeting, a bomb

The Haymarket Riot started when a bomb exploded.

was thrown, and at least seven people died. Police arrested eight labor leaders. They were tried in court and found guilty of starting a riot. Four of the leaders were hanged, one killed himself, and the other three were given life in prison. In 1893, Governor John Peter Altgeld decided that the court had not been fair in giving the men life in prison. He ordered the release of the three prisoners.

Another Illinois strike took place in 1888, this time against railroad companies. It started when the owners of several railroads decided to cut the pay of their workers. In return, workers refused to run the trains, so rail transportation came to a halt. Strikes in Illinois, particularly in Chicago, became common as more groups of workers started to form unions in their struggle to improve working conditions.

Immigrants and many other workers had similar problems. They were often poor, had little education, and struggled to feed their families. In 1889, Jane Addams and Ellen Gates Starr established Hull House in Chicago to help these families. At

Helping children was one of Jane Addams's main concerns.

Hull House, volunteers taught English, working women found housing, and poor people received food. Eventually, Hull House spread out to thirteen buildings where there were daycare centers and kindergartens, basic education, playgrounds, and gyms.

Life in Chicago wasn't all hard work. In 1893, the World's Columbian Exposition opened in Chicago and made that city famous throughout the world. The exposition displayed new inventions, modern scientific advances, and information about world cultures. The fair-

Visitors to the World's Columbian Exposition saw the first Ferris Wheel. It was 264 feet (81 m) tall.

grounds were lit by electric lights—a first for Chicago. Among the new inventions were the first zippers (called hookless fasteners) and the Ferris Wheel. About 27 million people came to see the exposition. This was a huge crowd, considering that the population of the entire United States was only about 63 million in 1890.

New York City, Washington, D.C., St. Louis, and Chicago had all competed for the right to hold the fair. However, Chicago's politicians talked so long and so loudly about their city that newspaper reporters called them "the windy politicians of Chicago." Chicago's nickname, the "windy city," comes from these politicians—not from the chilly winds that whip the city each winter.

TWENTIETH-CENTURY ILLINOIS

After the Civil War, slavery was abolished but conditions in the South for African-Americans remained poor. In the late 1800s and early 1900s many state governments passed laws, called Jim Crow laws, to keep African-Americans apart from Caucasians. African-Americans were barred from public restaurants, stores, rest rooms, theaters, and schools.

Many southern African-Americans wanted more for themselves and their families. They wanted good-paying jobs, better housing, and education for their children. Thousands of African-Americans decided to move from southern farms to northern cities where they thought they had better opportunities for themselves and their children. This shift was called the "great migration." African-Americans headed for factory

EXTRA! EXTRA!

After the Civil War, Batavia was called the "Windmill City." At that time, Batavia had three windmill companies that shipped their products to customers around the world.

jobs in Cairo, Springfield, and Chicago. Between 1900 and 1920, more than 100,000 African-Americans moved to Illinois.

Those who could afford to buy a ticket traveled on trains or by bus. In the South, African-Americans had to travel in "colored" sections—behind the coal car on trains or in the rear of a bus. O'Dell Wills remembers arriving in Cairo, Illinois, on the Greyhound bus:

"The driver said, 'You don't have to sit in the back anymore. We've crossed the Mason-Dixon line. You're free to sit where you want.' I sat in the front seat for the first time in my life."

By 1908, Springfield's African-American population was twice as large as it had been in 1900. Jobs were becoming scarce. Many white workers were angry that African-Americans held good-paying jobs that white workers wanted. People were on edge.

During the hot summer of 1908, two events occurred that helped start a riot. A white man was killed by an African-American, and a white woman said her African-American handyman had attacked her. These events caused a riot during which two African-American men were hanged, many were injured, and homes in the African-American section of town were set on fire. African-Americans fled to the local National Guard armory for safety. This incident—the Springfield Massacre—was one reason for the founding of the National Association for the Advancement of Colored People (NAACP), an organization that supports equal rights for all people.

While African-American minorities were struggling to gain some of their rights as citizens, women were finally achieving their right to vote.

In 1913, the Illinois state legislature passed a law that allowed women to vote—it was the first state east of the Mississippi River to allow women to vote in presidential elections. In the 1916 election, about 200,000 Illinois women marched to the polls to cast their votes. In 1919, the state legislature agreed to the Nineteenth Amendment of the U.S. Constitution, giving women all over the United States the right to vote. One group that worked hard for women's suffrage was the Woman's Christian Temperance Union. For a time this organization was headed by Frances E. Willard, an Illinois woman.

FIND OUT MORE

The NAACP has worked for equal rights for all people in the United States. In the beginning, they promoted an end to violence against African-Americans, better schools, and voter registration for African-Americans in the South, among other things. What problems do you think the NAACP should work on today?

THE WORLD AT WAR

When World War I (1914–1918) started, Illinois provided men and supplies for the war effort. Camp Grant near Rockford became a training site for new soldiers. The Great Lakes Naval Training Station near Chicago became the temporary home of 50,000 new sailors. By 1917, Illinois also had two military air bases. In all, the state sent 314,500 men to World War I, most in the army.

At home, meatpacking plants provided beef and pork for the military. Grain producers milled flour. Lead and steel were needed for building ships and tanks. With so many men overseas in the war, there were not enough workers to get the work done. In order to fill this need, northern

WHO'S WHO IN ILLINOIS?

Philip D. Armour (1832–1911), owner of a meatpacking company, developed ways to refrigerate meat products to protect them from spoiling.

This scene shows people boarding a double-decker bus in Chicago in 1926. A ride on the bus cost ten cents.

businesses placed notices in southern newspapers, encouraging African-Americans to come and fill these jobs. By 1920 the African-American population of Chicago, and Illinois in general, had doubled.

Wartime success and prosperity were short-lived. In 1929 the New York Stock Exchange crashed. When the stock market crashed, the United States was plunged into a terrible economic time. Many businesses shut down, factories and banks closed, and people lost their jobs. The country fell into a time during which many people could not afford food, clothing, or housing. This was called the Great Depression. In the early 1930s, more than 1.5 million people—one out of five people—in Illinois were out of work. Some local governments and churches took on the tough task of providing temporary housing, food, and clothing.

Towns of roughly built huts sprang up on public land. These towns were called "Hoovervilles" after President Herbert Hoover. Many people blamed Hoover for the hard times that people were having and the lack of jobs. Farmers struggled because prices for crops were very low. In addition, several years of low rainfall had turned much farmland into dry dust bowls.

Relief from the Great Depression arrived in the form of World War II (1939–1945). The war started when Germany and Italy attacked England and France. Now farmers had overseas markets for their crops. Companies could sell products made in Illinois to England and France, friends of the United States. The Caterpillar tractor plant in Peoria, for example, produced thousands of tank engines to send overseas.

In 1941 the war became truly a "world war" with the United States and its allies fighting against Germany and Italy in Europe and Japan in the Pacific. Over one million Illinois men and women joined the military, while others at home worked for the war effort in other ways. In 1942 at the University of Chicago, Enrico Fermi and his fellow scientists created the first nuclear (atomic) chain reaction. This discovery led to the first atomic bombs. These bombs were dropped on Hiroshima and Nagasaki, Japan, in August 1945. Atomic bombs caused a great deal of destruction to both cities. The use of these bombs forced Japan to surrender. World War II finally came to an end.

Enrico Fermi works in his laboratory at the University of Chicago.

Peace brought men and women home from the war. Again, the United States entered a period with plentiful jobs, successful businesses, and growth. By 1950, the state's population had reached 8,712,176. This decade showed great promise for Illinoisans. Gwendolyn Brooks, a Chicago poet, became the first African-American woman to win a Pulitzer Prize, a national award. A rather different "first" came to Des Plaines in 1954. That's where Ray Kroc opened the first McDonald's restaurant. Three years later, in 1957, the first U.S. nuclear power plant for making electricity opened in DuPage County. In 1959, the Chicago White Sox, a yearly loser in major league baseball, won the American League championship.

In Chicago, African-Americans faced growing problems. During the 1960s, many of the city's African-Americans lived in poor housing, yet paid high rent for their homes. They put up with rats in their hallways and crime on the streets. In winter, many had little or no heat. Many schools attended by African-Americans had broken toilets, cracked windows, and not enough books. At the same time, voters who lived in the downtown areas were not well represented in the city or state government.

Tension grew in the city. In July 1966, race riots broke out in the African-American section of Chicago. Rioters burned buildings and looted stores. Both whites and African-Americans were injured during the riots. The African-Americans were fighting to end *de facto segregation*.

WHO'S WHO IN ILLINOIS?

Gwendolyn Brooks (1917–2000) was an African American poet from Chicago. Among her best-known works are *Annie Allen* and *A Street in Bronzeville*.

Riots of another kind occurred in 1968. That year, the Democratic National Convention was held in Chicago. The convention was held to nominate a candidate in the presidential election. As the convention started, many young people protested against the war in Vietnam, which was going on at that time. When some of the protestors began to march for peace, police officers attacked the demonstrators and beat them with clubs. Some of the protestors threw rocks and bottles at officers. About 650 protestors were injured.

Politics in Illinois has changed with the times. In 1979, Jane Byrne became the first woman mayor of Chicago. Following Byrne as Chicago's mayor was Harold Washington, the first African-American to hold that job. Women in Illinois made further strides when Carole Moseley-Braun became the first African-American woman to be elected to the U.S. Senate.

In the 1990s, Illinois reorganized its state government and passed laws to provide new ways to pay for state programs, such as more money for schools. The state also began welfare reforms that put people on welfare to work. In 1999, the state government started a program called Illinois First. Through this program, the state will spend $12 billion in rebuilding roads and bridges.

EXTRA! EXTRA!

De facto segregation means separating people "by fact" rather than by law. The law doesn't segregate people. However, in reality groups of people may be segregated by where they are allowed to live. For example, landlords may refuse to rent apartments to African-Americans in a particular section of a town. When African-Americans live in one section of town, a public school for that area will have mostly African-American students. This is an example of *de facto segregation.*

Jane Byrne gives a victory sign after winning an election to become Chicago's first woman mayor.

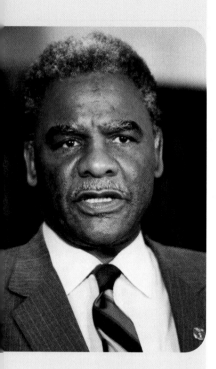

Harold Washington was elected as the first African-American mayor of Chicago.

In 2001, workers in Springfield started building the $115 million Abraham Lincoln Presidential Library and Museum. When it is complete, the museum will house the world's largest collection of items concerning Abraham Lincoln. Some of these items include his marriage license with Mary Todd, the earliest photograph of the president, and a rare copy of the Gettysburg Address written in his handwriting. Exhibits will tell the story of Lincoln.

Today's Illinois continues to be a transportation and industrial hub of the nation. Chicago's O'Hare Airport is one of the world's busiest airports, with flights leaving or arriving every two minutes. The state has ten interstates and twenty-two U.S. highways, as well as service from forty-five railroad lines. People in Illinois look to the future with pride as their state continues to be an industrial leader in the United States.

This view of Chicago shows Lake Shore Drive along Lake Michigan.

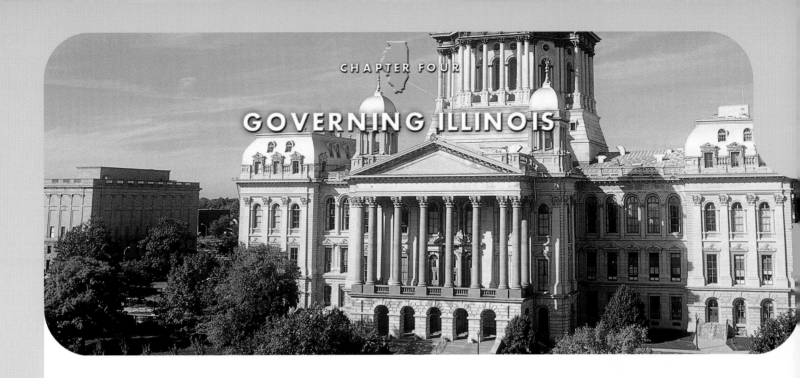

CHAPTER FOUR

GOVERNING ILLINOIS

The basis for governing Illinois is its constitution. Every state has a constitution, which sets down the rules and laws that run a government. The Illinois constitution lists the rights of the people living in the state and the powers of each branch of government.

The first Illinois constitution was written and adopted in 1818, when Illinois became a state. Since then, there have been several other constitutions and many changes, or amendments, to the constitution. The current constitution was adopted in 1970.

Amendments are suggested by the legislature or at a constitutional convention—a meeting held to talk about the constitution. When a change is suggested, the state's voters must approve the change before it becomes part of the constitution. The amendment must be passed by either three out of five people voting on the change, or by a majority (more than half) of the total number of people voting.

Springfield became the capital of Illinois in 1839. The capitol building was completed in 1888.

41

The Illinois government has three branches or parts: the executive branch, the legislative branch, and the judicial branch. These three branches balance the government so that no one branch has too much power. The executive branch makes sure state laws are enforced. The legislative branch makes new laws. The judicial branch—courts and judges—interpret the laws. The judicial branch decides if laws are fair or if someone accused of a crime is innocent or guilty.

THE EXECUTIVE BRANCH

The governor leads the executive branch. A lieutenant governor, an attorney general (the state's lawyer), a comptroller, and a secretary of state help the governor run the state. Voters elect these government officers every four years.

It is the governor's job to head all state government departments, such as education, agriculture, and transportation. The governor appoints people to run each department. He or she also creates a budget that tells the government how much money the state will spend each year and on which programs the state will spend money. The governor can also approve or reject bills (possible laws) passed by the state legislature.

THE LEGISLATIVE BRANCH

The legislature makes state laws. Illinois's lawmakers work in the 59-member Senate or the 118-member House of Representatives. The

ILLINOIS GOVERNORS

Name	Term	Name	Term
Shadrach Bond	1818–1822	John P. Altgeld	1893–1897
Edward Coles	1822–1826	John R. Tanner	1897–1901
Ninian Edwards	1826–1830	Richard Yates	1901–1905
John Reynolds	1830–1834	Charles S. Deneen	1905–1913
William L. D. Ewing	1834	Edward F. Dunne	1913–1917
Joseph Duncan	1834–1838	Frank O. Lowden	1917–1921
Thomas Carlin	1838–1842	Len Small	1921–1929
Thomas Ford	1842–1846	Louis L. Emmerson	1929–1933
Augustus C. French	1846–1853	Henry Horner	1933–1940
Joel Aldrich Matteson	1853–1857	John H. Stelle	1940–1941
William H. Bissell	1857–1860	Dwight H. Green	1941–1949
John Wood	1860–1861	Adlai E. Stevenson	1949–1953
Richard Yates	1861–1865	William G. Stratton	1953–1961
Richard J. Oglesby	1865–1869	Otto Kerner	1961–1968
John M. Palmer	1869–1873	Samuel H. Shapiro	1968–1969
Richard J. Oglesby	1873	Richard B. Ogilvie	1969–1973
John L. Beveridge	1873–1877	Daniel Walker	1973–1977
Shelby Moore Cullom	1877–1883	James R. Thompson	1977–1991
John M. Hamilton	1883–1885	Jim Edgar	1991–1999
Richard J. Oglesby	1885–1889	George H. Ryan	1999–
Joseph W. Fifer	1889–1893		

Senate and House of Representatives together are called the Illinois General Assembly. Senators serve four-year terms, and representatives serve two-year terms. State laws can cover almost any important topic, such as taxes, education, real estate, ecology, or crimes.

THE JUDICIAL BRANCH

The judicial branch in Illinois has more than 750 judges. The state's voters elect about four hundred judges. The governor appoints the other 350. The most powerful or highest court in Illinois is the State Supreme Court,

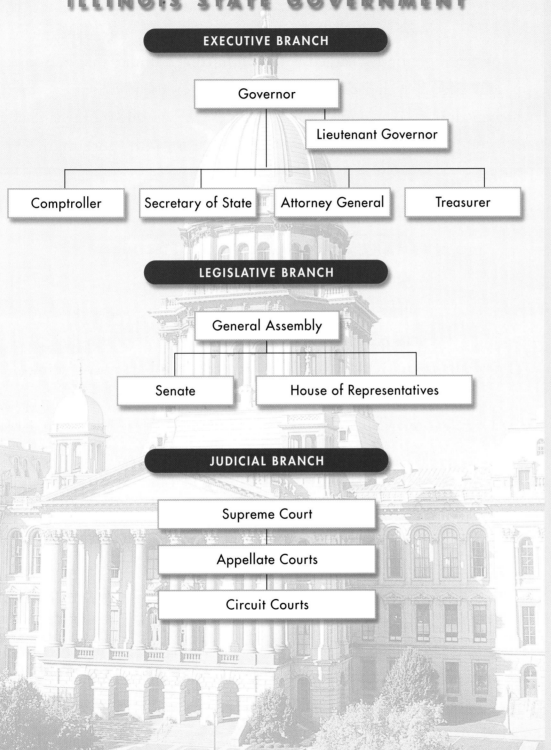

ILLINOIS STATE GOVERNMENT

EXECUTIVE BRANCH

Governor

Lieutenant Governor

Comptroller

Secretary of State

Attorney General

Treasurer

LEGISLATIVE BRANCH

General Assembly

Senate

House of Representatives

JUDICIAL BRANCH

Supreme Court

Appellate Courts

Circuit Courts

which has seven judges. The state's voters elect Supreme Court justices (judges). Lower courts include appellate courts and county circuit courts.

When a person is charged with committing a crime, that person is usually tried first in a circuit court. A case may then be appealed to a higher court. Cook County, which includes Chicago and more than half the state's people, has the largest circuit court with more than 175 judges.

TAKE A TOUR OF SPRINGFIELD, THE STATE CAPITAL

Springfield is where the state's business takes place. Besides the capitol building, the state offices and the governor's mansion are also there. The Old State Capitol building and the current capitol are only one block apart, in the center of the city.

The Old State Capitol cost $260,000 to build. It was used from late 1839 until 1876. Today, it is the home of the Illinois State Historical Library. In this library, you can read all about Illinois history, see old maps of the state, and study more than 1,500 documents written and signed by Abraham Lincoln.

Illinois's current capitol building cost $4,315,591 to build. It was started in 1868 and took twenty years to complete. The building is in the shape of a cross. At the center is a dome that reaches over 360 feet (110 m) high. The outer walls are made of limestone from Joliet and Lemont. The north and east pillars are made of granite. The grand staircase, the second floor columns, and floors are marble. The capitol's dome has a stained-glass skylight, where the image of the state seal is shown. The Illinois Senate, the House of Representatives, and the state executive branch have offices and meeting rooms in the capitol building.

Springfield was the Illinois home of Abraham Lincoln, perhaps the greatest President of the United States. There are plenty of "Lincoln" sights to see here. You can stop at the Great Western Railroad Depot (Lincoln Depot Museum) and imagine Abe Lincoln saying "goodbye" to his friends as he left to take office in Washington, D.C. You can visit Lincoln's old law offices. Lincoln and his law partners, Stephen Logan

Abraham Lincoln had his law office in this building on the downtown square.

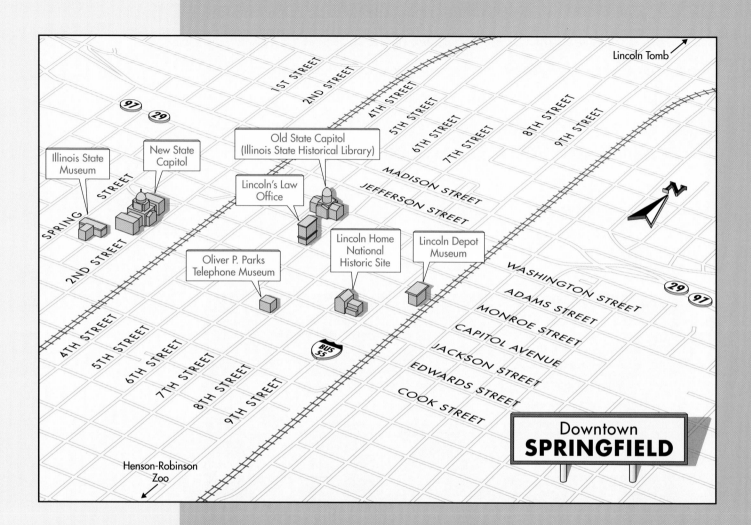

Lincoln Tomb

97 29

Illinois State Museum

New State Capitol

Old State Capitol
(Illinois State Historical Library)

Lincoln's Law Office

1ST STREET
2ND STREET
4TH STREET
5TH STREET
6TH STREET
7TH STREET
8TH STREET
9TH STREET

SPRING STREET

MADISON STREET

JEFFERSON STREET

Oliver P. Parks Telephone Museum

Lincoln Home National Historic Site

Lincoln Depot Museum

N

WASHINGTON STREET

ADAMS STREET

MONROE STREET

CAPITOL AVENUE

JACKSON STREET

EDWARDS STREET

COOK STREET

2ND STREET
4TH STREET
5TH STREET
6TH STREET
7TH STREET
8TH STREET
9TH STREET

BUS 55

29 97

Downtown
SPRINGFIELD

Henson-Robinson Zoo

and William Herndon, rented space on the third floor of a building that also housed a general store, the post office, and federal courtrooms. Nearby, you'll want to see the Lincoln Home National Historic Site, the actual house in which Lincoln lived while in Springfield. Lincoln bought the house for $1,200 in 1844 and lived in it for seventeen years. The furniture and decorations have been restored to look just as they would have in the 1860s.

Lincoln and his family lived in this home.

Once you've learned all about Lincoln, you'll want to see the rest of Springfield. The first thing you see as you enter the Illinois State Museum is a skeleton of one of the world's largest Ice Age mastodons. This museum has exhibits that cover about three hundred years of Illinois history and shows how people lived in Illinois over time, from Native American huts to sod houses to Chicago skyscrapers.

Visiting New Salem is like stepping back into the time when Lincoln lived there.

The Oliver P. Parks Telephone Museum has a fascinating collection of antique telephones. Some of these phones have no dials, just a crank handle used for calling the operator!

Don't forget to visit the Henson Robinson Zoo, which features rare and endangered species, such as Madagascar lemurs. There is a special site for nocturnal animals—animals that sleep all day and prowl at night. Stop by the penguin exhibit around feeding time to see these Antarctic acrobats playing in the water.

No visit to Springfield is complete without stopping in New Salem. A visit to this pioneer village takes you back in time to the 1830s. Abe Lincoln lived in New Salem from 1831 to 1837 and worked as the settlement's postmaster. He also clerked in a store, worked as a surveyor, studied law, and fought in the Black Hawk War. You'll see timber houses, shops, and stores as history comes alive. New Salem is a living museum—actors dress and act like the people who lived and worked there more than 150 years ago.

CHAPTER FIVE

THE PEOPLE AND PLACES OF ILLINOIS

A full house at Wrigley Field, home of the Chicago Cubs, means almost 40,000 people!

Today, **12,419,293 people** (2000 census) live in Illinois. For every 100 Illinoisans, 74 are Caucasian and 15 are African-American. The state also has a large number of Hispanics, as well as Asians. Across the state, the population density is 223 people per square mile. In Chicago, the population density is about 11,930 people per square mile (4,606 per sq km). That's crowded!

Where Did They Come From?

Illinois's people have varied, interesting backgrounds. Many African-Americans trace their ancestry to free Africans and escaped slaves who came into Illinois during and after the Civil War. Others have families that moved into Illinois during the Great Migration. The early European settlers to Fulton were Dutch, and many of Moline's settlers were from France. Germans settled in Des Plaines. Swedes farmed the land around Bishop Hill. Festivals such as Fulton's Dutch Days and Bishop Hill's Jordbruksdagarna, a Swedish fair, link today's Illinoisans to their heritage.

FIND OUT MORE

Population density is the number of people in a given area. Figure out the population density of your classroom. First find out the area of the room. Then, compare it to the number of people in your class. What do you come up with?

Arcola, just east of Springfield, has a large Amish community. The Amish are a group of Protestants who live in tight-knit communities. They avoid modern conveniences, such as cars, radios, and telephones. Instead, they use traditional horse-drawn carriages, sew their clothes by hand, and cook in wood-burning stoves. Arcola is the heart

An African-American family celebrates Kwanzaa.

of broomcorn country, and Amish craftspeople make and sell these brooms, along with homemade quilts, pies, fresh baked breads, and other woodcrafts.

Since settlers first came to Illinois, the state has grown by welcoming immigrants. Today, Chicago attracts "settlers" from other countries. More than 50,000 people from Guatemala, a country in Central America, live in Chicago. About three out of ten of the city's foreign-born residents are Mexican, and another one in ten are from Poland. On the whole, Illinois's foreign-born population equals almost one-tenth of the state's population.

Tempting pastries crowd a tray in this Polish bakery.

Illinois grows more pumpkins for processing than any other state. Ask an adult to help make the delicious pumpkin custard recipe below.

PUMPKIN CUSTARD
(Yields eight servings)

1 15-oz. can pumpkin
1/2 cup granulated sugar
1/4 cup brown sugar
1 teaspoon cinnamon
1/2 teaspoon ground ginger
1/2 teaspoon salt
1/4 teaspoon cloves
1/4 teaspoon nutmeg
3 eggs
1 can evaporated milk

Here's what to do:
1. Put all ingredients in a bowl and mix until smooth.
2. Spray the inside of a one-quart ovenproof bowl with pan coating spray.
3. Pour in the custard mix.
4. Bake at 350°F for fifty minutes. Custard is done when a butter knife is inserted in the center and comes out clean.
5. Cool and serve with whipped cream. Refrigerate the remaining custard.

Stars Shine in Illinois

Illinois has had more than its share of famous people. Poets from Illinois include Gwendolyn Brooks, Shel Silverstein, and Carl Sandburg. Other Illinois writers are Ernest Hemingway and Saul Bellow. You see Illinois talent on TV and in movies from Roseanne and Robin Williams to Oprah Winfrey. We hear Illinois's gifted musicians on radio or CDs. These include gospel singer Mahalia Jackson, composer Quincy Jones, and jazz musician Miles Davis.

Sports heroes are also in the spotlight in Illinois. For many years Hall of Fame football player Walter Payton thrilled fans of the Chicago Bears with his brilliant end runs. On the ice, speed skater Bonnie Blair from Champaign won a record-breaking five Olympic gold medals. Track and field athlete Jackie Joyner Kersey, another Olympic medal winner, also comes from Illinois. Joyner Kersey has long been considered one of the world's top women athletes.

Of course, the Chicago Bulls basketball team wowed the country in the 1990s, winning the National Basketball Association championship six times. Led by Michael Jordan and Scottie Pippen, the Bulls won titles in 1991, 1992, 1993, 1996, 1997, and 1998.

Education in Illinois

Education has always been important in Illinois. The first school in the state was built in Cahokia in 1784. Today, Illinois has nearly two million students in its public and private elementary and secondary schools. This is the fifth largest number of students in the United States.

Illinois is noted for its excellent colleges and universities. Among the outstanding schools of higher education in the state are Northwestern University, Bradley University, DePaul University, Eureka College, Southern Illinois University, and nearly eighty others. Of special interest is the Native American College that teaches tribal culture, including Native American history, language, and literature. Through these courses of study, the college hopes to keep the heritage of native people alive.

Michael Jordan led the Chicago Bulls to a series of championships.

EXTRA! EXTRA!

In the 1990s the Illinois license plate on Michael Jordan's car read: RARE AIR.

WISCONSIN

IOWA

MICHIGAN

Lake
Michigan

Freeport

Rockford

Waukegan

Chicago

Peoria

Champaign

Urbana

Decatur

Springfield

INDIANA

MISSOURI

N

Carbondale

KENTUCKY

	Beef		Hogs
	Chemicals		Oil
	Coal		Potatoes
	Corn		Poultry
	Dairy cattle		Soybeans
	Food processing		Stone
			Wheat

0   30   60 mi.
0   30   60 km

Illinois is an interesting mix of industry and agriculture, mining and manufacturing. Almost half of all workers find jobs in service industries. They're employed in health care, restaurants, hotels, and schools. Store and warehouse employees amount to two out of ten workers. About two out of ten workers are in manufacturing, and one in ten works for the government. Although Illinois has long been an agricultural leader, only two in one hundred workers are found on farms.

Raising hogs is just one kind of farming in Illinois.

Illinois has about 80,000 farms and 28.3 million acres of farmed land. In all, agriculture adds $4 billion to the state's overall production each year. The main farm products are corn, soybeans, oats, wheat, orchard fruits, and hay. Beef cattle, dairy farming, and hog farming are also common, with hogs being the most important.

Across the state, manufacturing is strong. Factories produce electrical equipment, farm machinery, food processing, printing, and chemicals. The main manufacturing centers are Chicago, Rock Island, Moline, and East Rock Island. Many well-known companies have their main offices in Illinois—Sara Lee, Caterpillar, Rand McNally, Motorola, State Farm Insurance, Sears Roebuck, Ameritech, Walgreen, John Deere, Ace Hardware, and Quaker Oats.

A worker inspects an antenna at the top of a skyscraper.

In the southern region, mining is an important industry. Coal mines are found near East St. Louis, Carbondale, La Harpe, Champaign, and Jacksonville. Oil wells are found in the southern half of the state. Peat, crushed stone, sand, clay, and gravel are also mined.

Another important industry in Illinois is tourism. Chicago is a popular city for business meetings and weekend trips. Lake Michigan and the Chain O'Lakes area provide boating, fishing, and swimming in summer months. In addition, festivals and events take place every week throughout the state.

The number and variety of industries in Illinois provide a strong economy. The state is a leader in both manufacturing and agriculture.

TAKE A TOUR OF ILLINOIS

If you tour Illinois, plan two separate trips: one to Chicago and one to the rest of the state. There is much to see and plenty to do, so let's get busy.

People in Chicago love parades. This scene is from a Mexican Pride parade.

In Chicago, there are museums, music, theater, events, and adventure awaiting you. If you love parades, Chicago is the place for you, with more than two hundred parades each year. The largest parades are on St. Patrick's Day (March 17), Columbus Day (October 12), and Thanksgiving. These colorful parades usually feature floats, bands, movie and TV stars, and gigantic balloons in the shape of cartoon characters.

The main tourist attraction in Chicago is Navy Pier. This is the place where aircraft carriers once docked during World Wars I and II. Covering 50 acres, the pier features the Chicago Children's Museum, the Chicago Shakespeare Theater, and many shops and restaurants. At the Chicago Children's Museum, you can learn more about great historical

inventions and how they helped to solve problems. You can even try to create your own invention at the Inventing Lab. Navy Pier also has a 150-foot-high (45-m) Ferris wheel, with forty cars that can hold six people each. At night the Ferris wheel's forty spokes blaze with thousands of lights. From the top of this giant Ferris wheel you catch a fantastic view of Lake Michigan and the Chicago skyline.

You can also get a great view of the Chicago skyline and four states from the enclosed Skydeck on the 103rd floor of the Sears Tower. At that point you are 1,353 feet (412 m) above the streets of Chicago. The Sears Tower is one of the world's tallest skyscrapers at 1,450 feet (442 m) high. An antenna on top brings it to a height of 1,730 feet (527 m). Twenty-two radio and television stations broadcast from the tower antennas.

While you're in Chicago, you can't miss the John G. Shedd Aquarium where more than 6,000 freshwater and saltwater animals live. You can dive into the underwater world of beluga whales, Pacific whitesided dolphins, harbor seals, and penguins. The Oceanarium, next to the aquarium, is considered the world's largest indoor marine-mammal pavilion. Check out the whale and dolphin shows in Whale Harbor.

Just around the corner from the aquarium, you'll find the Adler Planetarium with exhibits about timepieces, telescopes, and space travel. The Adler's StarRider Theater is a realistic space journey, while the Sky Show presents programs about stars and planets.

EXTRA! EXTRA!

The Sears Tower weighs about 222,500 tons. It is covered by more than 28 acres of aluminum.

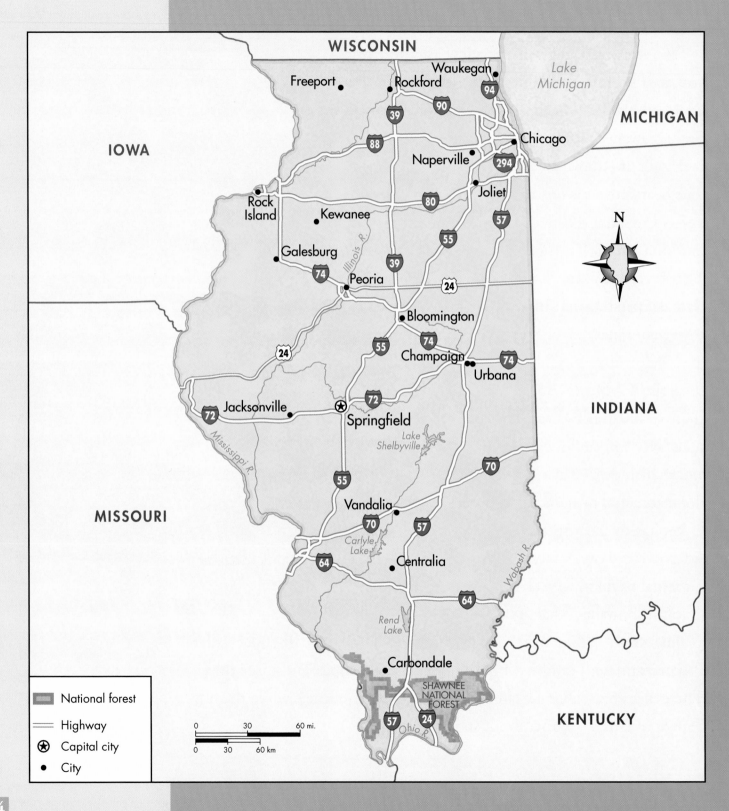

WISCONSIN

Freeport

Waukegan

Rockford

94

90

39

Lake
Michigan

MICHIGAN

IOWA

88

Chicago

Naperville

294

Rock
Island

Kewanee

80

Joliet

57

55

Galesburg

Illinois R.

N

74

39

Peoria

24

Bloomington

55

74

24

Champaign

Jacksonville

72

72

Springfield

Urbana

74

INDIANA

Mississippi R.

Lake
Shelbyville

70

55

70

Vandalia

70

57

MISSOURI

Carlyle
Lake

Wabash R.

64

Centralia

64

Rend
Lake

Carbondale

SHAWNEE
NATIONAL
FOREST

KENTUCKY

57

24

Ohio R.

National forest

Highway

Capital city

City

0   30   60 mi.

0   30   60 km

A short walk from the planetarium will bring you to The Field Museum. This museum houses 19 million artifacts. The Field Museum covers natural sciences, which are studies of humans, animals, plants, and the Earth. You'll find Sue, the fossil remains of a *Tyrannosaurus rex*, at the Field. Sue is the largest and best-preserved *Tyrannosaurus rex* skeleton in the world. Named for Sue Hendrickson, the scientist who found the skeleton, Sue has a skull that weighs a ton. The dinosaur's teeth are as long as your arm! Another exhibit describes ancient Egyptians and how they made mummies. Yet another exhibit shrinks you to the size of a bug and allows you to explore an underground world. Together, The Field Museum, Adler Planetarium, and the Aquarium attract more visitors each year than anywhere else in Chicago.

The Museum of Science and Industry's hands-on exhibits give you a chance to ride down into a coal mine. You can experience traveling in a German submarine during World War II. You can get behind the controls of an F-14 Tomcat military jet and pretend to fly it. If space travel sends chills down your spine, be sure to visit the Henry Crown Space Center and Omnimax Theater to learn about astronauts and space travel. You can see the actual *Apollo 8* spacecraft that orbited the moon. In one exhibit you can take a ride in a pretend space shuttle and experience how astronauts feel when a real space shuttle takes off. Tighten your seatbelts! You're in for the ride of a lifetime.

EXTRA! EXTRA!

The Great Chicago Fire of 1871 burned at the rate of 65 acres an hour. The only two public buildings to survive were the Old Water Tower and its pumping station. The pumping station now serves as a visitor information center.

For sports fans, Chicago has the Bulls basketball team, the Bears football team, and the White Sox and Cubs baseball teams. If you'd rather play yourself, the city has hockey and ice skating rinks, sailing and swimming, public parks, and tennis.

When you are in Chicago, there is one experience you just can't miss—Chicago deep-dish pizza. It's difficult to find a pizza parlor without this taste sensation on its menu.

The White Sox often play on the diamond at Comiskey Park.

Illinois From Top to Toe

Begin your Illinois tour in Rockford, near the Wisconsin border. This is the home of the Burpee Seed Company, one of the world's largest garden seed and plant companies. The town features many beautiful gardens. You can walk through the public gardens or take tours of many private gardens. Then, visit the Burpee Museum of Natural History on Main Street. You can learn all about Native American culture, plus minerals and fossils. The museum has a very realistic coal forest—complete with thunderstorms. Bring your umbrella! Rockford's Discovery Center Museum is another hands-on science and technology spot geared for children. You can take part in electronic and mechanical exhibits, and learn about how machines work.

About a 45-minute drive from Chicago, near Gurnee, is Six Flags Great America. This theme park features rides, theaters, shops, and restaurants. Take a ride on the Iron Wolf, a stand-up roller coaster that is just one of ten roller coasters in the park. Riders on the Raging Bull roller coaster fall two hundred feet (61 m) into an underground cavern.

A family visit to Nauvoo, a Mormon town, is well worthwhile. The town features Joseph Smith's home, completely restored. There is also a red brick store, much like an 1840s general store. Check out the kinds of things that your great-great-great-great-great grandparents bought way back when they were young. You might even buy a peppermint stick for yourself.

Just south of East St. Louis, the Cahokia Mounds State Historic Site has sixty-five mounds, many of which were built more than one thousand years ago. Think about the work involved in building these mounds. There were no bulldozers or earthmovers in those days. All the soil was dug by hand, carried in small, woven baskets, and piled up to create these huge earthworks. It's hard to believe that more than a thousand years ago, at least 100,000 people lived near this site, but it is true. They had families and friends, just like you.

Work in a stop at the Brookfield Zoo, which covers 215 acres. More than two thousand animals live there in their natural habitats. The exhibits help you to understand the importance of saving the environment. You can visit Tropic World, which

EXTRA! EXTRA!

Champaign and Urbana are twin cities. They are separated by one street.

EXTRA! EXTRA!

The town of Lincoln is the only town named for Lincoln before he became U.S. President. As a lawyer, Lincoln prepared the court documents that allowed the settlement's developers to sell lots. In return for this favor, the developers named it after him.

This historical site preserves the remains of mounds built by ancient people.

has rainstorms. In the Living Coast exhibit, you can travel alongside the exhibit, beneath water level, and see how a coastal habitat is formed. You can also enjoy a swamp, a salt creek wilderness, and Habitat Africa. The Fragile Kingdom exhibit shows you exactly how much animals depend on their habitats to survive.

Arcola is located not far from Springfield. Arcola is at the northern border of what was once known as the Broomcorn Belt. This area was named for broomcorn, a type of corn that is used in making brooms. It has a finer leaf and bushier tassel than other kinds of corn. There's an Amish community just west of town where you can buy homemade quilts and crafts. You can also stop in the Illinois Amish Interpretive

Center. Here, you can learn more about the Amish way of life and watch a short video about the Old Order Amish. Displays feature horse-drawn buggies and traditional Amish clothing.

Finally, no trip to Illinois would be complete without a stop in Metropolis. This town calls itself "Superman's hometown," after the cartoon hero who is from Metropolis. Every day in Metropolis, the daily *Planet* prints a newspaper with information about town events. The Super Museum features information about the famed comic hero.

ILLINOIS ALMANAC

Statehood date and number: December 3, 1818, the 21st state

State seal: An American eagle in the center, holding a banner with the state motto. Below the eagle is a red, white, and blue shield, representing the original thirteen colonies. Olive branches on either side of the shield symbolize peace.

State flag: A white background with the state seal on it, and the word "Illinois." Adopted: 1915; state name added, 1969.

Geographic center: Logan, 28 miles (45 km) northeast of Springfield

Total area/rank: 57,918 square miles (150,007 sq km); rank, 25th

Borders: Indiana, Kentucky, Missouri, Iowa, Wisconsin, Lake Michigan

Latitude and longitude: From 36°58' to 42°30' N and 87°30' to 91°30' W

Highest/lowest elevation: Charles Mound, 1,235 feet (376 m)/On Mississippi River, 279 feet (85 m)

Hottest/coldest temperature: 117°F (47°C), East St. Louis, July 14, 1954/-36°F (-38°C), Congerville, January 5, 1999

Land area/rank: 55,593 square miles (143,985 sq km); rank, 24th

Inland water area/rank: 750 square miles (1,942 sq km); rank, 17th

Population/rank: 12,419,293 (2000 census), 5th

Population distribution: 85 percent urban, 15 percent rural

Origin of state name: French version of *illiniwek*, meaning, "strong men" or "the people"

State capital: Springfield

Counties: 102

State government: 59 senators; 118 representatives

Major rivers, lakes:
Rivers: Mississippi, Illinois, Wabash, Chicago, Des Plaines, Rock, Ohio, Fox, Sangamon, Kankakee, Green, Kaskaskia

Lakes: Michigan, Carlyle, Crab Orchard, Rend, Chain O'Lakes

Farming products: Corn, soybeans, wheat, oats, hay, apples, peaches,

pumpkins, potatoes, hogs, cattle, dairy products, chickens, turkeys, eggs, sheep/lambs, minks

Manufacturing products: Heavy construction machinery, printed material, farm machinery, electrical instruments, appliances, iron and steel, processed foods, meat products, railroad equipment, chemicals, pharmaceuticals

Mining products:

Bituminous coal, petroleum, natural gas, fluorspar, zinc, copper, lead, lime, silver, barite, clay, sand and gravel, crushed stone

Average annual precipitation: 38 inches (97 cm)

Bird: Cardinal

Fish: Bluegill

Flower: Violet

Fossil: Tully monster

Insect: Monarch butterfly

Mineral: Fluorite

Motto: State Sovereignty, National Union

Nickname: The Prairie State, Land of Lincoln

State fairs: Springfield (mid-August), DuQuoin (Labor Day weekend)

Song: "Illinois." Words by Charles H. Chamberlain. Music by Archibald Johnson. Adopted: 1925

Tree: White oak

TIMELINE

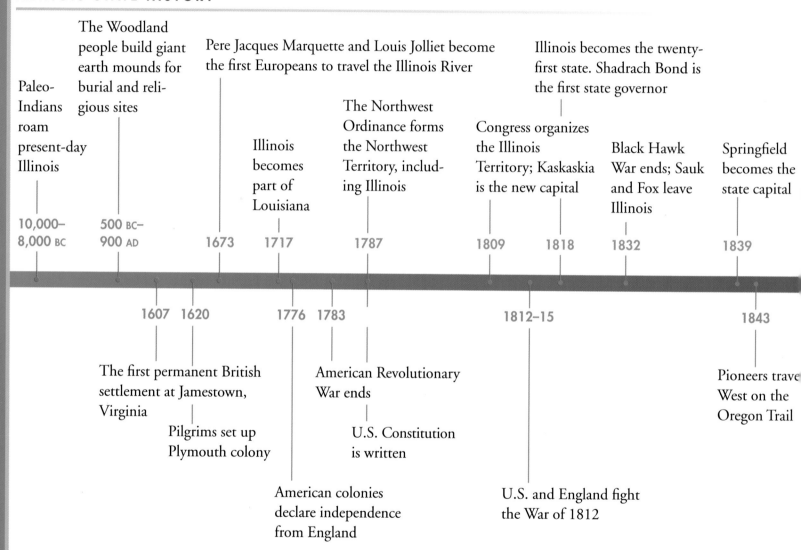

Paleo-Indians roam present-day Illinois
10,000–8,000 BC

The Woodland people build giant earth mounds for burial and religious sites
500 BC–900 AD

Pere Jacques Marquette and Louis Jolliet become the first Europeans to travel the Illinois River
1673

Illinois becomes part of Louisiana
1717

The Northwest Ordinance forms the Northwest Territory, including Illinois
1787

Congress organizes the Illinois Territory; Kaskaskia is the new capital
1809

Illinois becomes the twenty-first state. Shadrach Bond is the first state governor
1818

Black Hawk War ends; Sauk and Fox leave Illinois
1832

Springfield becomes the state capital
1839

1607
The first permanent British settlement at Jamestown, Virginia

1620
Pilgrims set up Plymouth colony

1776
American colonies declare independence from England

1783
American Revolutionary War ends
U.S. Constitution is written

1812–15
U.S. and England fight the War of 1812

1843
Pioneers travel West on the Oregon Trail

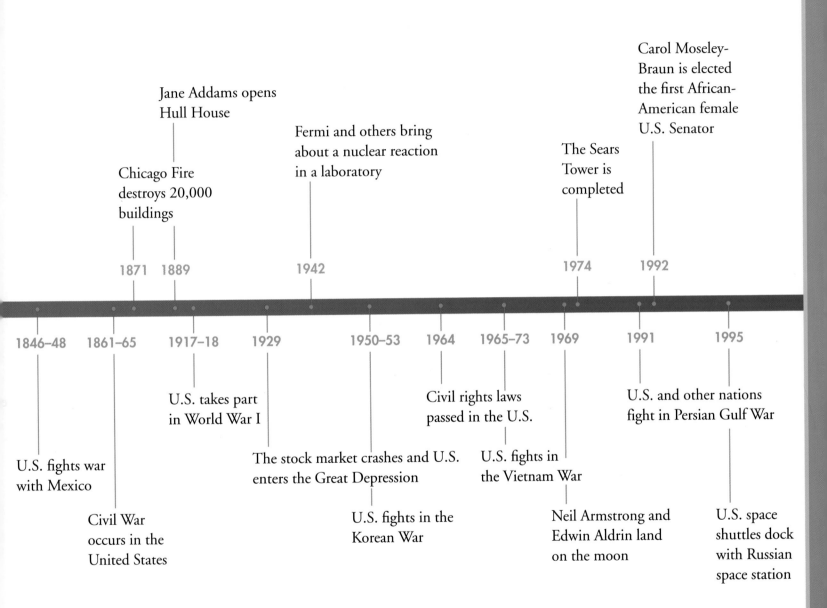

Jane Addams opens
Hull House

Chicago Fire
destroys 20,000
buildings

Fermi and others bring
about a nuclear reaction
in a laboratory

The Sears
Tower is
completed

Carol Moseley-
Braun is elected
the first African-
American female
U.S. Senator

1871   1889   1942   1974   1992

1846–48   1861–65   1917–18   1929   1950–53   1964   1965–73   1969   1991   1995

U.S. takes part
in World War I

Civil rights laws
passed in the U.S.

U.S. and other nations
fight in Persian Gulf War

U.S. fights war
with Mexico

The stock market crashes and U.S.
enters the Great Depression

U.S. fights in
the Vietnam War

Civil War
occurs in the
United States

U.S. fights in the
Korean War

Neil Armstrong and
Edwin Aldrin land
on the moon

U.S. space
shuttles dock
with Russian
space station

GALLERY OF FAMOUS ILLINOISANS

Jane Addams
(1860–1935)
Founder of Hull House, a social reformer, and winner of the Nobel Peace Prize.

Gwendolyn Brooks
(1917–2000)
Award-winning African-American poet. In 1968, Brooks was named poet laureate of Illinois.

Enrico Fermi
(1901–1954)
Scientist and part of the team that discovered how to produce an atomic reaction.

Ulysses S. Grant
(1822–1885)
Leader of the Union army during the Civil War and eighteenth president of the United States. Lived in Galena.

Quincy Jones
(1933–)
A composer, conductor, and trumpeter, Jones has won countless awards for his music. Born in Chicago.

Michael Jordan
(1963–)
Although born in Brooklyn, New York, Michael Jordan rose to international fame on the Chicago Bulls basketball team.

Ronald Reagan
(1911–)
Former president of the United States, California governor, and popular movie and television actor. Born in Tampico.

Carol Moseley-Braun
(1947–)
The first African-American woman elected to the U.S. Senate (1992). Born in Chicago.

Harold Washington
(1922–1987)
The first African-American mayor of Chicago.

Oprah Winfrey
(1954–)
Born in Mississippi, Winfrey makes Chicago her home. Noted African-American author, television host, movie actress.

GLOSSARY

abolish: to put an end to something

amendment: a change in a law or document

capital: the city that is the center of a state or country government

capitol: the building in which a government meets

climate: an area's average weather conditions

constitution: basic rules and laws that run a government

economy: how people make money

executive: the group that runs a state or government

governor: an elected person who leads the state

immigrants: people who move from one country to live in another country

interpret: to translate or to explain

judicial: judges and courts

labor union: group of workers who join together to demand better pay and safer working conditions

legislature: a group of people who make laws

manufacturing: making products, such as cars or lamps

molten: hot, melted

Paleo-Indians: early or "old" native people

population: the number and mix of people in a region

reservoir: an artificial lake, usually created when a dam is built

strike: when workers refuse to work

suffrage: the right to vote

tourism: businesses that provide hotels, restaurants, and entertainment for visitors

transportation: a system of roads, trains, buses, and airports

FOR MORE INFORMATION

Web sites

The State of Illinois
http://www.state.il.us/
Information about the state.

State Symbols
http://www.museum.state.il.us/exhibits/symbols
Symbols of Illinois.

Museum of Science and Industry
http://www.msichicago.org
Some of the museum's most popular attractions are highlighted.

Books

Harness, Cheryl. *Abe Lincoln Goes to Washington, 1837–1865.* Washington, D.C.: National Geographic Society, 1997.

Sandburg, Carl. *The Sandburg Treasury: Prose and Poetry for Young People.* New York: Harcourt Brace Jovanovich, 1970.

Simon, Charnan. *Jane Addams: Pioneer Social Worker.* Danbury: Children's Press. 1998

Addresses

Chicago Office of Tourism
78 E. Washington Street
Chicago, IL 60602

Illinois Bureau of Tourism
620 E. Adams Street
Springfield, IL 62701

Springfield Convention and Visitors Bureau
109 N. Seventh St.
Springfield, IL 62701

INDEX

MEET THE AUTHOR

Barbara A. Somervill has visited Chicago many times, usually on business. The Field Museum and the Shedd Aquarium are two of her favorite Chicago spots. To write this book she used the Internet, called Chambers of Commerce and tourist bureaus, and visited the local library. Barbara was raised and educated in New York state. She's also lived in Toronto, Canada; Canberra, Australia; Palo Alto, California; and Simpsonville, South Carolina.